VOLCANOES AND EARTHQUAKES

By Joanna Brundle

KidHaven PUBLISHING

TRANSFORMING EARTH'S GEOGRAPHY

Published in 2018 by
KidHaven Publishing, an Imprint of Greenhaven Publishing, LLC
353 3rd Avenue
Suite 255
New York, NY 10010

Designer: Natalie Carr
Editor: Grace Jones

Photo credits: Abbreviations: l-left, r-right, b-bottom, t-top, c-centrer, m-middle. Front Cover – Wead. 2 – Fotos593. 4 – Dutourdumonde Photography. 5 – Lucky Team Studio. 6ml – EQRoy. 7t – Wead. 7b – Ikunl. 8 – Johan Swanepoel. 9b – CHEN WS. 10mr – Rainer Albiez. 11m – arindambanerjee. 12t – Wildnerdpix. 12b – Budkov Denis. 13t – Marco Regalia. 13m – Marisa Estivill. 13b – SidEcuador. 14t – George Burba. 14b - MarcelClemens. 15t - Jon Frank. 15b - Matteo Chinellato. 16m - albund. 17tl - sspopov. 18mr - photo story. 18bl - Leonard Zhukovsky. 19b – Sthaporn Kamlanghan. 20bl – Everett Historical. 20br – Everett Historical. 21mr – A.S. Zain. 23m – yankane. 23b – paulaphoto. 24t – Sailorr. 24b – Porojnicu Stelian. 25 – Photovolcanica.com. 26mr – Aaron Rutten. 26b – Cameron Cross. 27 – J. Helgason. 28bl – f11photo. 28br – Alla Laurent. 29tr – Ti Santi. 29b – Jag_cz. 30m – Tristan3D. Images are courtesy of Shutterstock.com, with thanks to Getty Images, Thinkstock Photo, and iStockphoto.

Cataloging-in-Publication Data

Names: Brundle, Joanna.
Title: Volcanoes and earthquakes / Joanna Brundle.
Description: New York : KidHaven Publishing, 2018. | Series: Transforming Earth's geography | Includes index.
Identifiers: ISBN 9781534524972 (pbk.) | 9781534524170 (library bound) | ISBN 9781534524989 (6 pack) | ISBN 9781534524187 (ebook)
Subjects: LCSH: Earthquakes–Juvenile literature. | Volcanoes–Juvenile literature.
Classification: LCC QE521.3 B78 2018 | DDC 551.2–dc23

Printed in the United States of America

CPSIA compliance information: Batch #CW18KL: For further information contact Greenhaven Publishing LLC, New York, New York at 1-844-317-7404.

Please visit our website, www.greenhavenpublishing.com. For a free color catalog of all our high-quality books, call toll free 1-844-317-7404 or fax 1-844-317-7405.

VOLCANOES AND EARTHQUAKES

CONTENTS

Words that look like **this** can be found in the Glossary on page 31.

WHAT ARE EARTHQUAKES?

Imagine! The ground is rumbling under your feet. Suddenly, it starts to jerk violently from side to side or up and down. Buildings are shaking and starting to crumble. The road beside you cracks and splits. It's an earthquake!

Earthquakes are common, occurring somewhere in the world about twice every minute. Every year around 100 of these cause damage, but most last less than a minute.

A catastrophic earthquake hit Kathmandu, Nepal, on April 26, 2015. It killed nearly 9,000 people.

The point where an earthquake happens, under the surface of the earth, is called the focus. The epicenter is the place on the surface of the earth that is directly above the focus. It is generally the place that shakes the most. Energy blasts out from the focus in the form of shock waves, similar to ripples when you throw a stone into a puddle. These shock waves are called seismic waves, and they can travel for thousands of miles. Seismic waves that travel along the earth's surface are called surface waves.

Earthquakes can cause other natural disasters, such as landslides, avalanches, and flooding. These natural events can kill many people.

Smaller tremors often happen before and after the main shock of an earthquake. Those that happen before the main shock are called foreshocks, and those that happen after it are called aftershocks.

As of 2017, the deadliest earthquake that ever occurred happened in China in 1556. Around 830,000 people were killed.

WHAT ARE VOLCANOES?

Deep within the earth lies hot **molten** rock called magma. Magma is full of gas bubbles and is less **dense** than the rock above it. Being lighter, it tries to rise above the solid rock and to escape by breaking through the earth's surface. Volcanoes are places where it **erupts**.

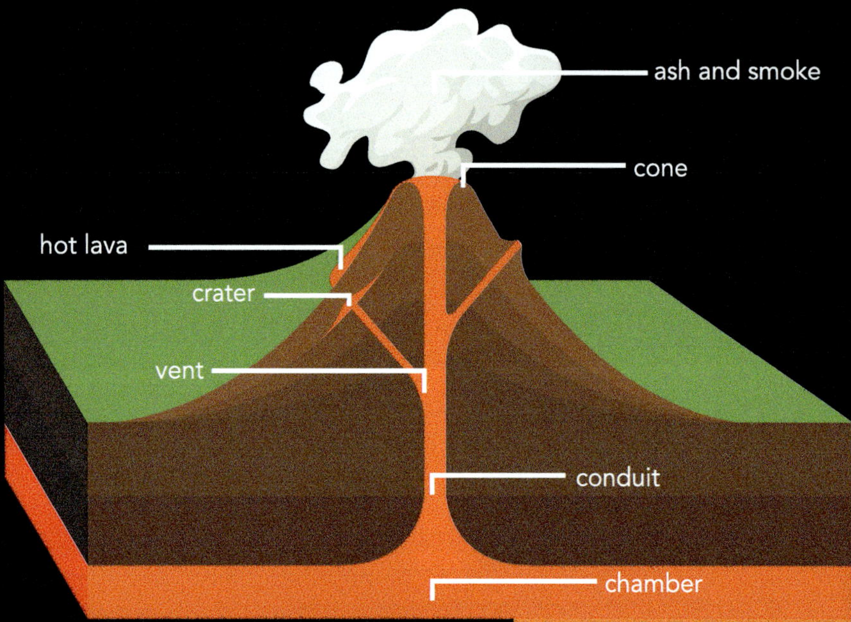

Magma from the chamber pushes up the conduit and out of the vent. At the surface, it is called lava. As the hot lava flows downhill, it cools and forms a cone.

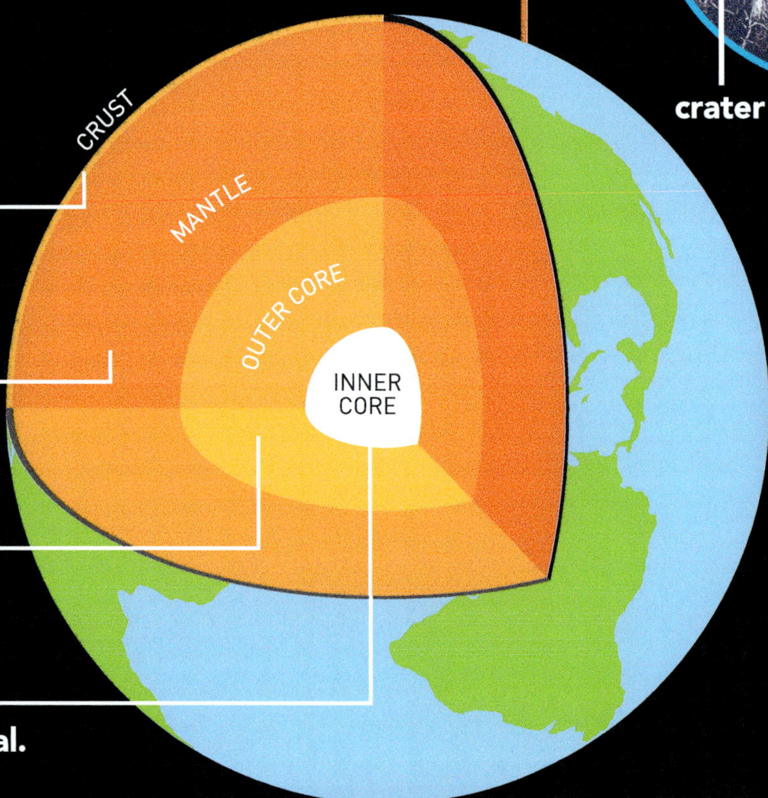

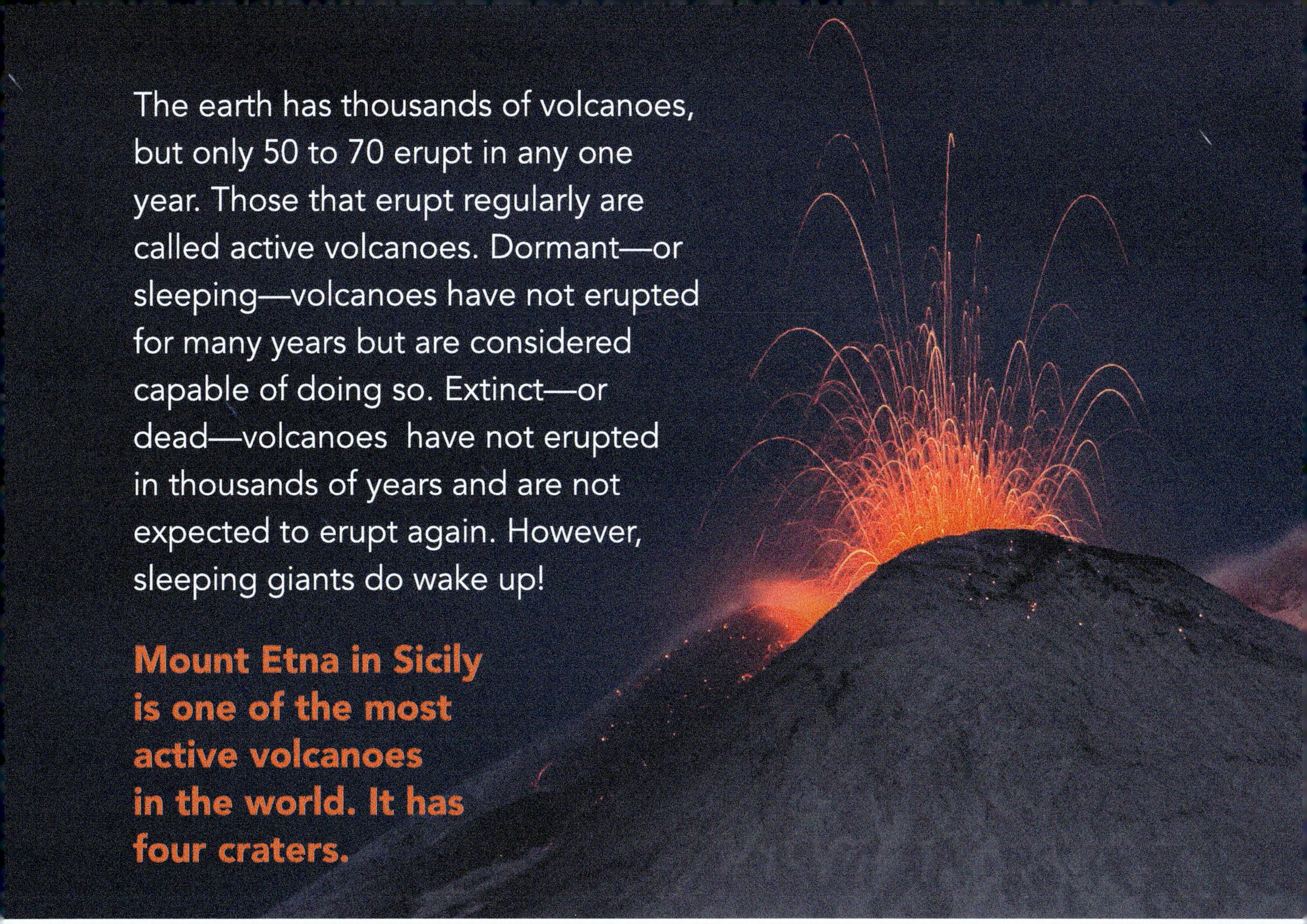

The earth has thousands of volcanoes, but only 50 to 70 erupt in any one year. Those that erupt regularly are called active volcanoes. Dormant—or sleeping—volcanoes have not erupted for many years but are considered capable of doing so. Extinct—or dead—volcanoes have not erupted in thousands of years and are not expected to erupt again. However, sleeping giants do wake up!

Mount Etna in Sicily is one of the most active volcanoes in the world. It has four craters.

Mount Fuji in Japan last erupted in 1707 and is considered dormant.

WHAT CAUSES EARTHQUAKES AND VOLCANOES?

The outer layer of the earth—the crust—is like a giant jigsaw puzzle made up of huge slabs of rock. It feels solid under our feet, doesn't it? In fact, the giant slabs, called tectonic plates, are constantly moving as they ride on top of the layer of molten rock underneath. They move slowly, at about the same rate as your fingernails grow. That's up to 2.4 inches (6 cm) a year.

If the earth was the size of an apple, the crust would be thinner than the apple's skin.

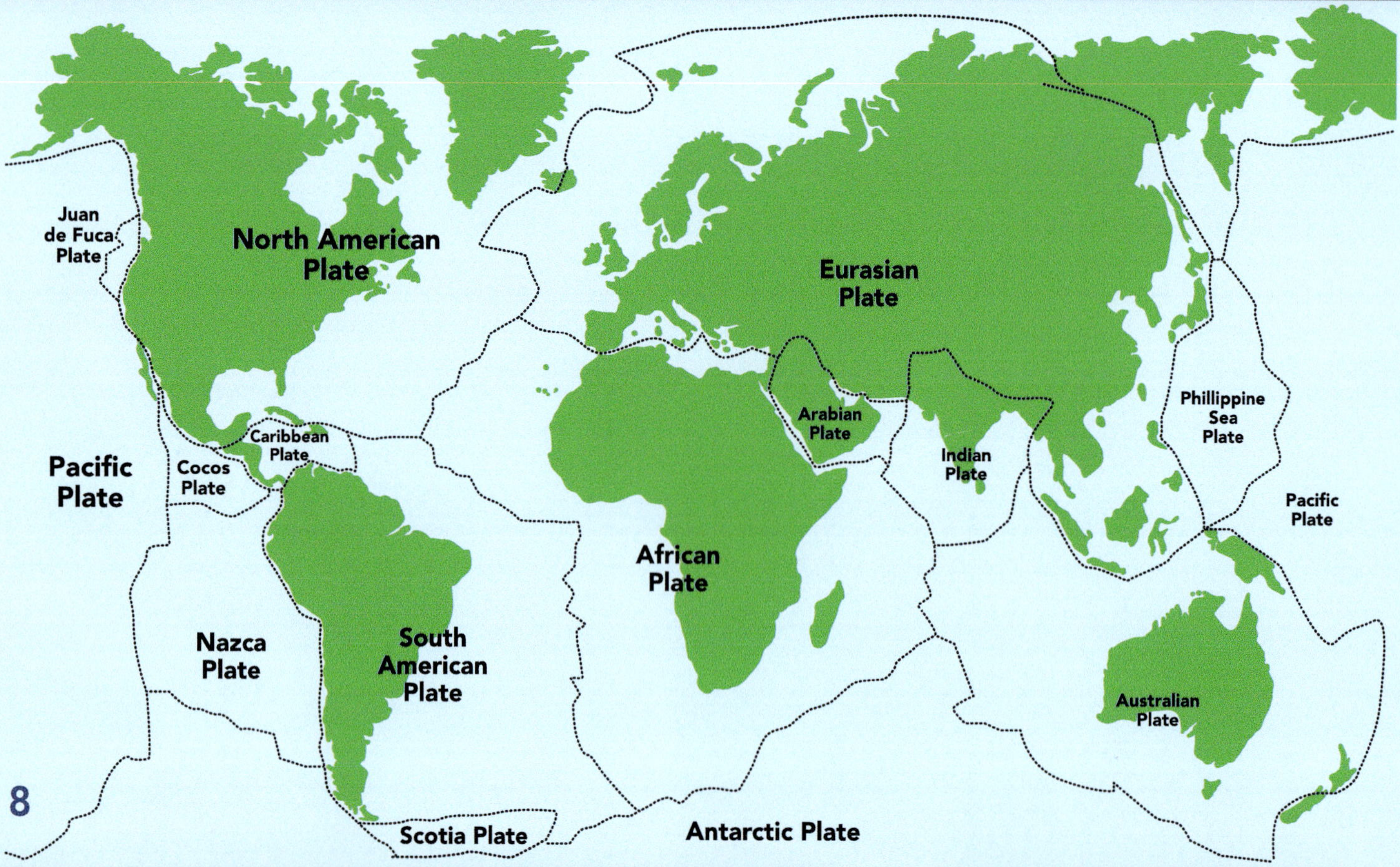

As they move, tectonic plates come together in different ways. They may meet head on, grind sideways against one another, pull apart, or slip underneath each other. The moving plates create huge amounts of pressure, which can cause cracks on the earth's surface called faults or fault lines.

The San Andreas Fault in California is about 30 million years old and is about 808 miles (1,300 km) long. You can see it from space, and it marks where the North American Plate meets the Pacific Plate.

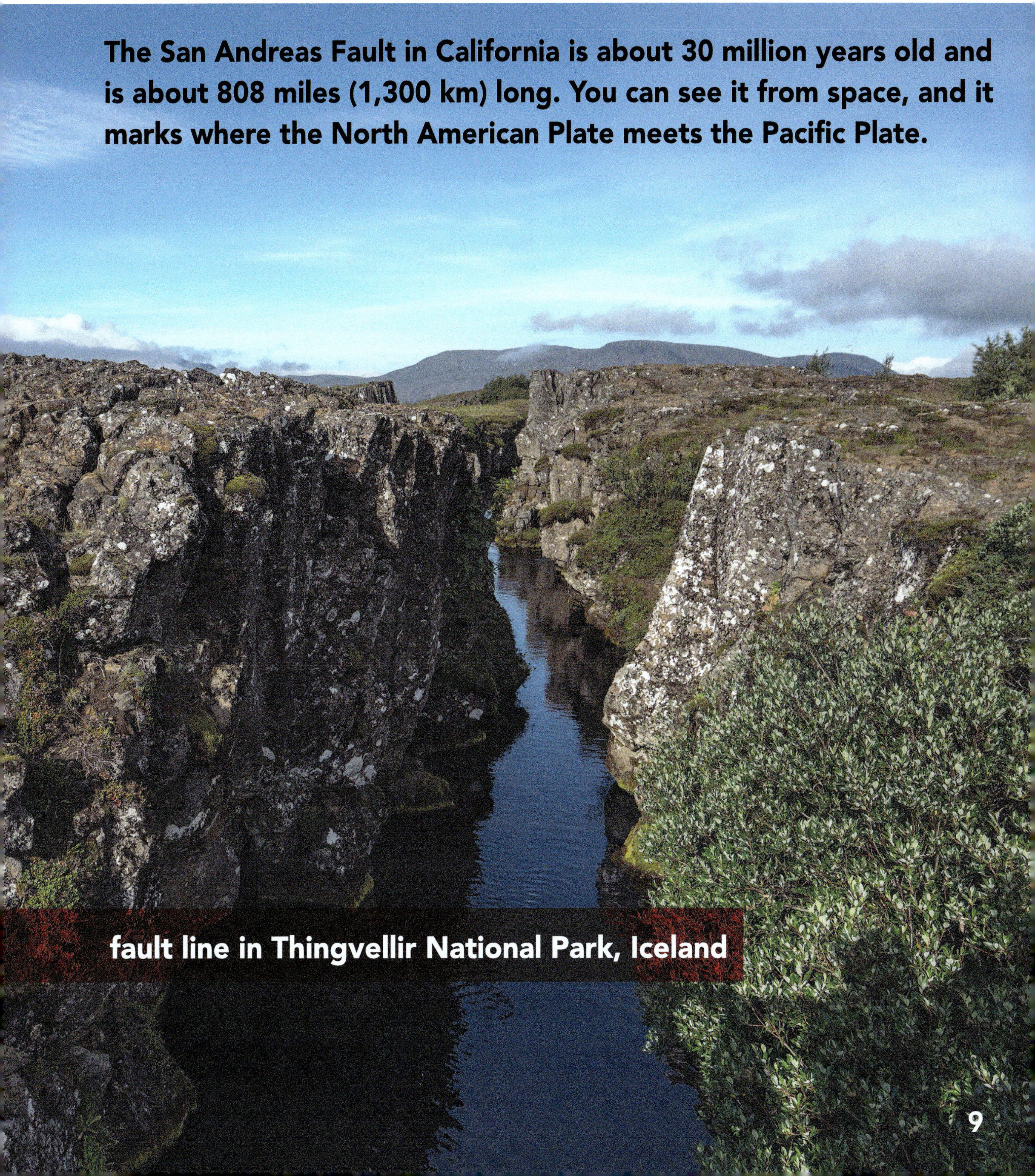

fault line in Thingvellir National Park, Iceland

Plate boundaries are areas where plates come together. Most volcanoes are formed along plate boundaries. Some occur where magma rises up to fill a gap caused by plates pulling apart. Sometimes, one plate sinking and melting beneath another causes an eruption. However, not all volcanoes form along plate boundaries. Hot spots are places where magma forces its way through the middle of a tectonic plate.

Volcanic eruptions at a hot spot in the Pacific Plate formed the islands of Hawaii. These islands form a chain because, while the plate kept moving, the place where the super-hot magma spewed out was not moving.

All around the edge of the Pacific Ocean are plate boundaries where the Pacific Plate meets other plates. There are so many volcanoes in this region that it is known as the "Ring of Fire."

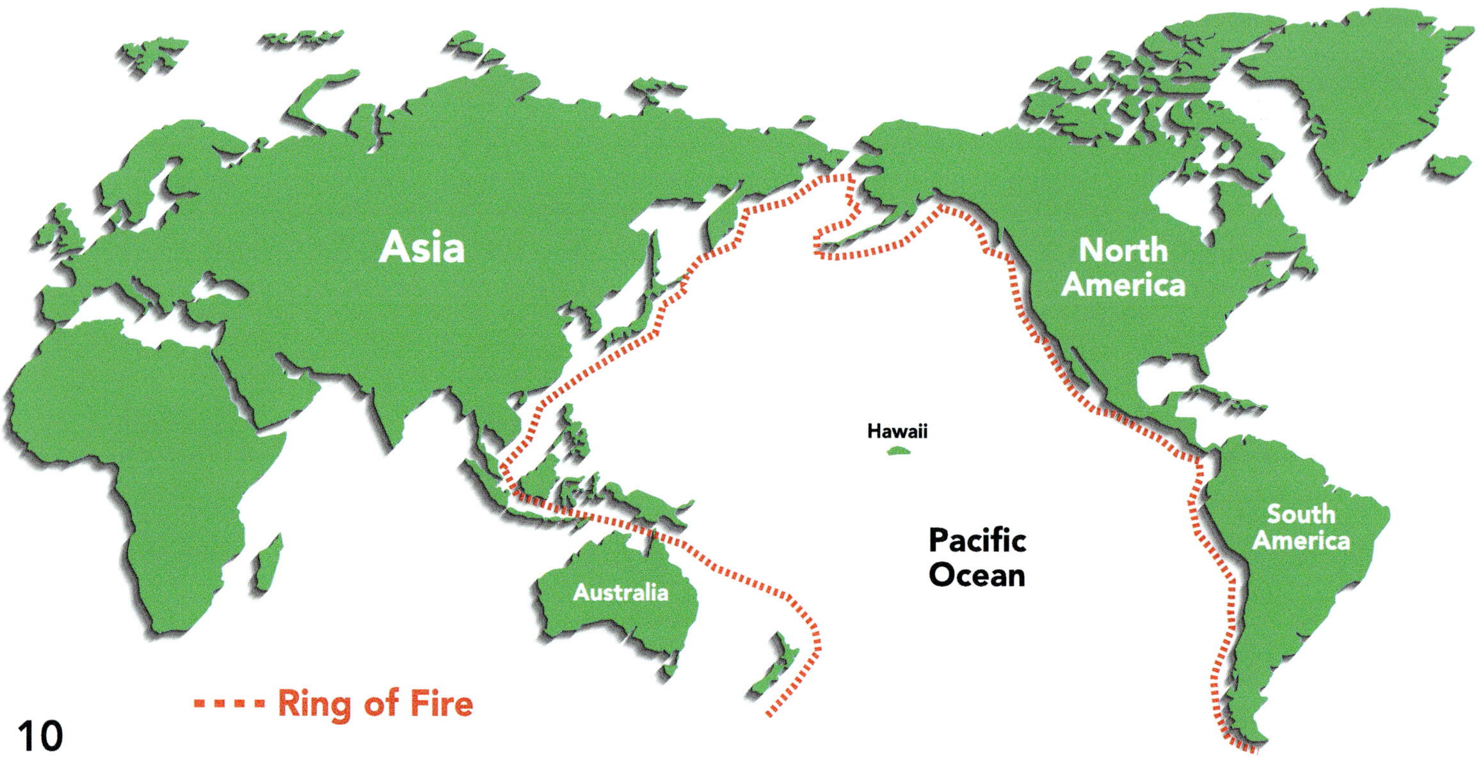

Scientists know that most earthquakes occur along fault lines. The force applied by tectonic plates that are moving causes huge amounts of rock along a fault line to slip suddenly and violently. When this happens, the energy is released as shock waves that make the ground shake. Think of pushing your hands together to snap a stick. Pressure builds, the stick breaks, and you can feel shock waves up your arm.

Haiti is a poor country that suffered a serious earthquake in 2010. Poorly constructed buildings collapsed, and around 230,000 people died. Fewer people die in earthquakes in wealthier countries, where safer but more expensive building materials are used.

THREE KINDS OF FAULTS

01 **NORMAL FAULT** Top layer of crust moves down.

02 **REVERSE FAULT** Plates squeeze together. Top layer of crust moves up.

03 **STRIKE-SLIP FAULT** Blocks of rock grind past one another.

DIFFERENT KINDS OF VOLCANOES

Mauna Loa, a shield volcano in Hawaii, is the world's largest active volcano.

The shape of a volcano depends on the type of volcanic material that it spews out. Magma can be thin and runny or thick and sticky, depending on the temperature of the molten rock as well as the gases and **minerals** inside it. Shield volcanoes form when fast-flowing, runny lava spreads out over a wide area, forming a gently sloping mountain.

Cinder cone volcanoes form when lumps of sticky magma erupt violently into the air. The lumps cool into cinders and pile up to form small, steep volcanoes.

Strato—or composite—volcanoes are tall, pointed cones made up of layers of cooled lava and ash.

Popocatépetl, also called El Popo, is an active stratovolcano in Mexico.

Sometimes a volcano erupts so violently that the magma chamber is emptied. The volcano collapses in on itself, leaving a hollow, ring-shaped crater called a caldera. A crater lake is a caldera that has filled with water.

The Quilotoa caldera is in the Andes mountain range in South America.

Many volcanoes erupt under the sea. The water causes the lava to cool quickly, and the volcano keeps growing until it reaches the surface, forming a volcanic island.

The Galápagos Islands were formed from undersea volcanoes, which are called seamounts.

VOLCANIC MATERIAL

pahoehoe lava

Black smokers are dark, smoky jets of water that form around underwater volcanoes. Small particles build up to form tall, black chimneys.

Some kinds of lava have unusual names. As it cools, thin, runny pahoehoe lava forms a wrinkled skin that looks like coils of rope. Thick, sticky aa lava is spiky and jagged. When underwater volcanoes erupt, the cooling action of the water forms smooth, rounded pillow lava.

Pele's hair lava is made up of thin strands of volcanic glass. It is named after Pele, the Hawaiian goddess of volcanoes.

Pele's hair lava

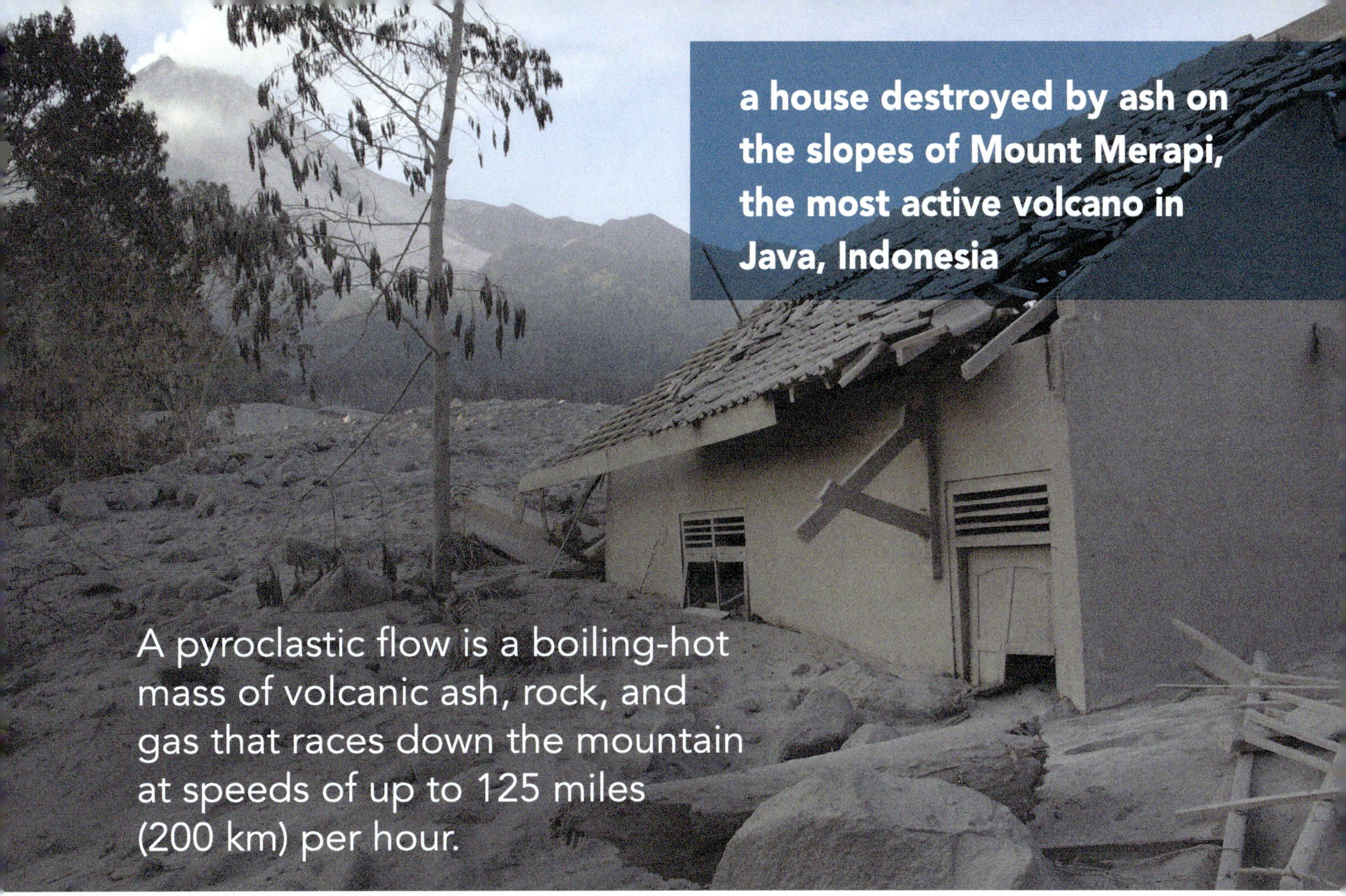

a house destroyed by ash on the slopes of Mount Merapi, the most active volcano in Java, Indonesia

A pyroclastic flow is a boiling-hot mass of volcanic ash, rock, and gas that races down the mountain at speeds of up to 125 miles (200 km) per hour.

Volcanoes do not erupt mud, but a mudslide is one of the greatest dangers of an eruption. Mudslides—or lahars—form when water, either from heavy rain or snow melted by a pyroclastic flow, mixes with volcanic ash and dust.

Sometimes, as molten lava cools to form rock, the minerals inside it form precious crystals, such as diamonds.

MEASURING EARTHQUAKES AND VOLCANOES

Seismologists are scientists who study earthquakes. They use equipment called seismographs and information from **satellites** to see where the tectonic plates are moving and where an earthquake may happen.

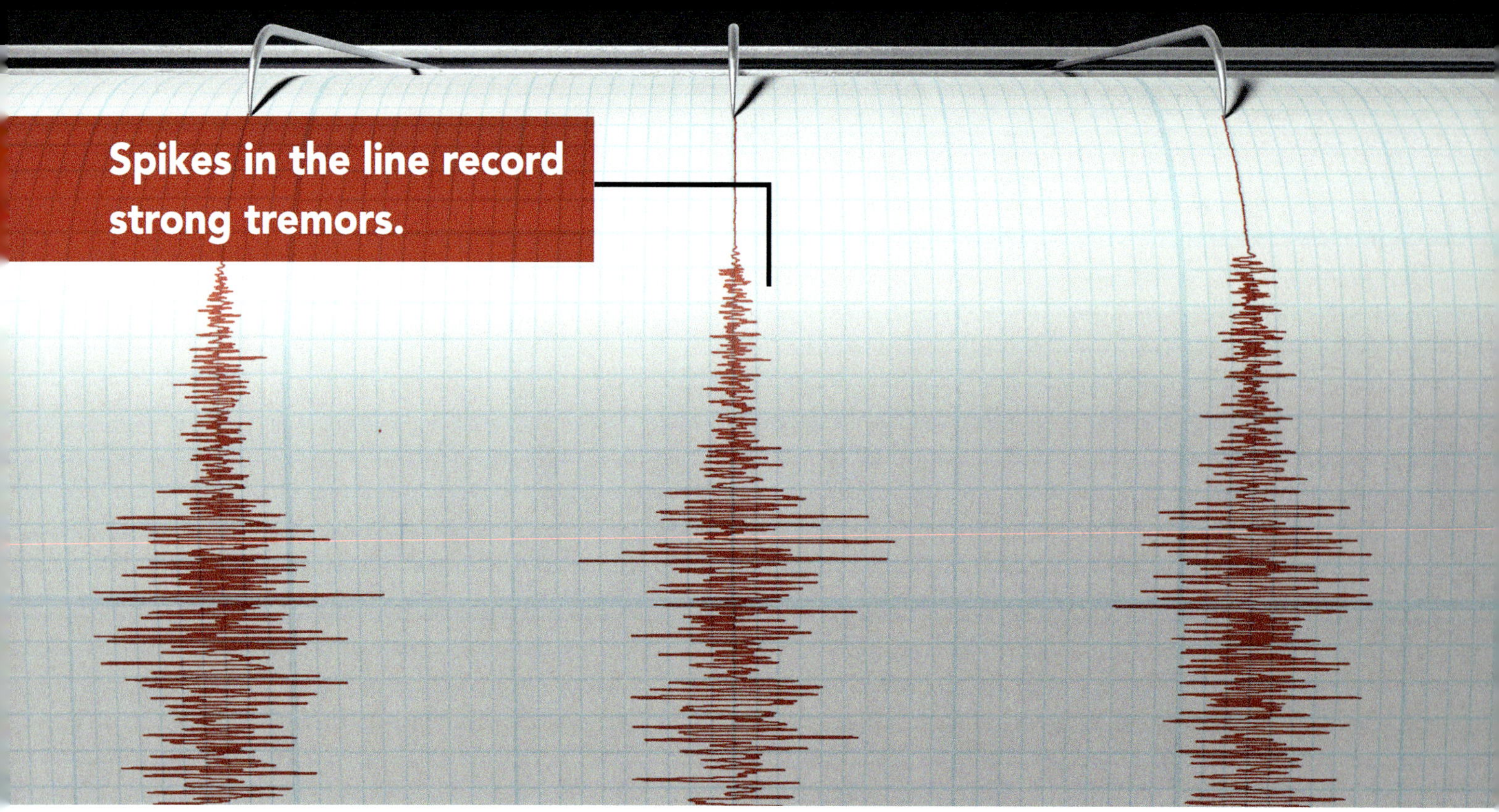

Spikes in the line record strong tremors.

Scientists use the Richter Scale and the Moment Magnitude Scale to measure the strength of earthquakes. The higher the number is, the stronger the earthquake.

A seven or more on the Richter Scale is a major earthquake. The Mercalli Scale describes what people experience during an earthquake. For example, a four means parked cars rock from side to side.

Scientists who study volcanoes are called volcanologists. As well as working in laboratories, they visit volcano sites, sometimes while the volcano is actually erupting. It's dangerous work! Wearing goggles, masks, and special suits such as this to protect them from the heat, they collect gas and lava samples.

A supervolcano is a massive eruption. Yellowstone National Park is the site of a supervolcano that last erupted 640,000 years ago. It spewed out enough ash and gas to block out the sun and plunge the world into darkness. Scientists think it could erupt again—but not in our lifetime.

Volcanologists use the Volcanic Explosivity Index, or VEI, to measure volcanoes. A supervolcano scores eight.

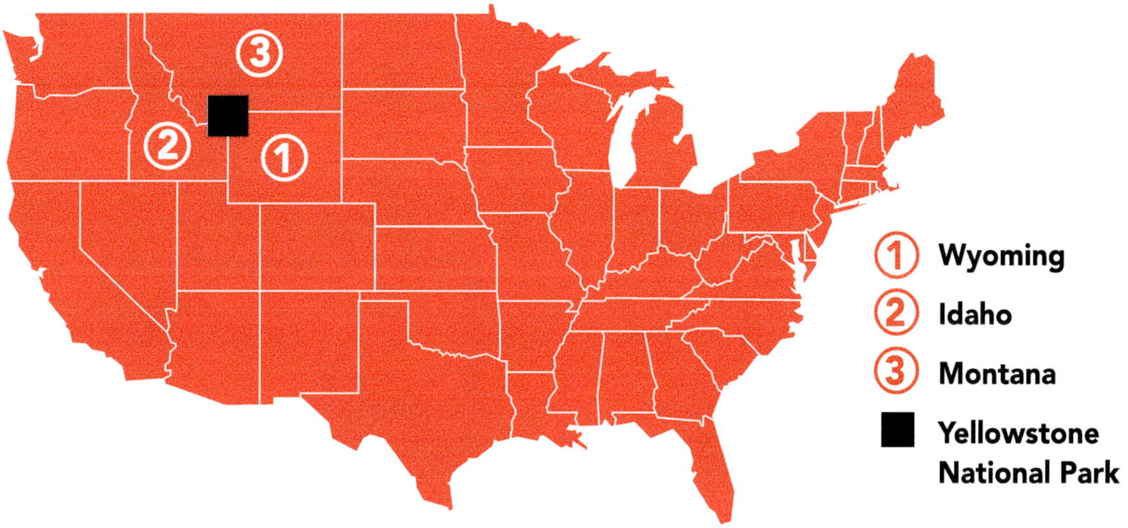

SURVIVING EARTHQUAKES AND VOLCANOES

Buildings in earthquake zones can be built to withstand the shaking of an earthquake. Layers of rubber and steel between the buildings and their foundations absorb shock waves, just like your sneakers when you run. Steel beams strengthen walls and reduce the amount of shaking. Upper floors that can sway a little help to stop buildings collapsing by changing some of the earthquake's energy into movement.

Following an earthquake, rescue teams are often helped by search dogs who are trained to smell people buried under the wreckage.

The rubber pads in the base of the Transamerica Pyramid in San Francisco helped it to survive a large earthquake in 1989.

Children practice this drill in earthquake regions.

HOW TO SURVIVE A VOLCANO

01 Evacuate your area as quickly as possible if you are told to do so. Don't stop to collect your belongings.

02 Stay upwind of a volcano to protect yourself from ash and poisonous gases.

03 Wear a mask or goggles, and cover your skin.

04 Stay away from any channels, such as river valleys, where lava might collect.

05 Volcanic lakes may contain enough acid to burn your skin, so don't swim in them!

an acidic crater lake in the Philippines

THE SAN FRANCISCO EARTHQUAKE, 1906

San Francisco, California, stands on two fault lines—the San Andreas Fault and the Hayward Fault. In 1906, it was a busy trading city, second only to New York City. But on April 18, a huge earthquake, measuring 8.2 on the Richter Scale, struck. The main shock lasted over a minute. Fires started as broken electrical wires sparked, and soon the city was engulfed in flames. Around 3,000 people died and 300,000 people lost their homes.

San Francisco on fire after the earthquake

City hall was destroyed.

THE INDIAN OCEAN TSUNAMI, 2004

A tsunami is a series of waves caused by volcanic eruptions or earthquakes under the sea. As the fast-moving waves approach land, they slow down and gain height, causing disastrous damage as they crash onto the shore.

The Indian Ocean tsunami was caused by a violent earthquake that happened out at sea. The waves caused by the earthquake were 50 feet (15 m) high when they hit the land and traveled at speeds of up to 497 miles (800 km) per hour.

COUNTRIES WORST AFFECTED BY THE TSUNAMI

1. Indonesia
2. Malaysia
3. Thailand
4. Sri Lanka
5. India
6. Bangladesh
7. Myanmar
8. Kenya
9. Tanzania
10. Somalia
11. Seychelles
12. Maldives

● earthquake epicenter

tsunami damage in Aceh, Indonesia

The tsunami made 2 million people homeless.

CATASTROPHE IN JAPAN, 2011

Japan sits on a fault line where the Pacific and Eurasian tectonic plates meet. It is well prepared for earthquakes, but the force of the earthquake which struck on March 11, 2011, caught everyone by surprise. Measuring a massive 9.0 on the Richter Scale, it happened 80 miles (130 km) off the coast, but was strong enough to rock buildings in Tokyo, 230 miles (370 km) away.

The earthquake was so powerful that a satellite in space was able to detect vibrations from it.

The earthquake was the largest ever recorded in Japan.

A tsunami, triggered by the earthquake, hit Japan and traveled up to 6 miles (10 km) inland. More than 15,000 people died. Things got even worse when the tsunami hit the Fukushima **nuclear plant** and damaged the cooling system. A massive explosion in one of the reactors followed, which caused dangerous **radioactive** leaks. Around 300,000 people were evacuated. It is believed that the Fukushima area will not be safe to go to until at least 2021—10 years after the radioactive leaks.

The tsunami tossed cars, homes, and boats around like toys.

This little girl is wearing a mask to try to protect her from radioactive dust.

HISTORIC ERUPTIONS: VESUVIUS, TAMBORA, AND KRAKATOA

Mount Vesuvius in Italy was thought to be an extinct volcano when it erupted in August of AD 79. A loud boom was quickly followed by hot ash raining down. A pyroclastic flow then completely buried the town of Pompeii and its inhabitants in a layer of rock, ash, and cinders, 23 feet (7 m) deep. The nearby town of Herculaneum was also buried. Pompeii, which had been preserved by the layer of ash, was uncovered by **archaeologists** 1,700 years later.

Decayed bodies left hollows in the hardened ash. Casts of the bodies were made by filling the hollows with plaster.

A volcanic eruption blew apart the Indonesian island of Krakatoa in 1883, triggering tsunami waves 131 feet (40 m) high. In 1930, a new island appeared, formed by an undersea volcano. It is called Anak Krakatoa, meaning "Child of Krakatoa."

Anak Krakatoa erupts several times a day and is growing by 22 feet (6.8 m) a year.

So much ash was thrown into the sky by the eruption of Mount Tambora in Indonesia in 1815 that the sun was blocked out, which caused temperatures to go down around the world.

The gloom caused by Tambora's eruption is thought to have inspired the spooky tale of Frankenstein, written by Mary Shelley.

MOUNT ST. HELENS AND EYJAFJALLAJÖKULL

Mount St. Helens is a stratovolcano in the state of Washington. In 1980, it was shaken by a series of earthquakes, triggering the largest landslide in history at the time. The side of the mountain bulged before the explosive eruption that followed completely blasted away its north side, leaving a massive, jagged crater. Deadly lahars, formed from melting snow and rivers of hot ash, flattened vast areas of forest.

The eruption changed the shape of the mountain from this ...

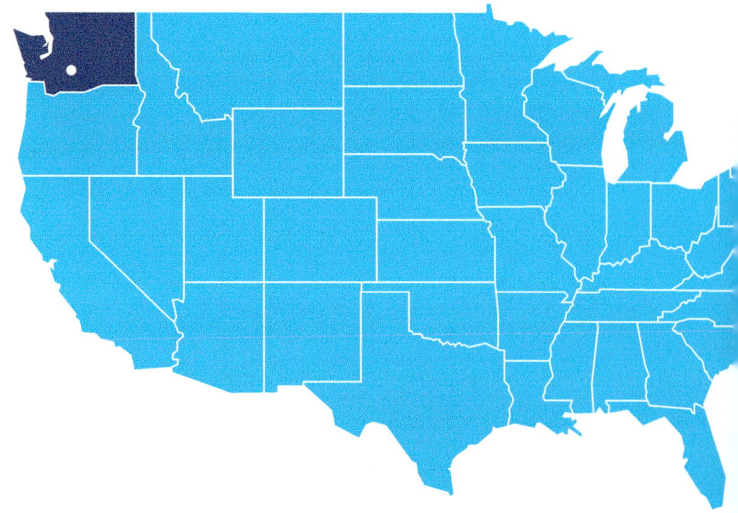

... to this.

Eyjafjallajökull is the name of a **glacier** that sits on top of a volcano in Iceland. In April 2010, after a series of earthquakes in the region, the volcano erupted. Spewing magma melted the glacier and released gigantic ash clouds, large enough to darken the skies over much of Europe. Ash clouds contain small, rough particles that can clog jet engines, so flights were canceled and many people were stranded.

ash clouds released by Eyjafjallajökull

Flights to and from Europe were canceled.

FASCINATING FACTS

01 The word "volcano" comes from Vulcan, the Roman god of fire. He was believed to live on Mount Etna.

02 There are some advantages to living near a volcano. The minerals in volcanic ash help crops to grow well. Magma heats underground water, which bursts to the surface as geysers and hot springs, where people enjoy swimming. Hydrothermal (hot water) power stations use these geysers to provide cheap, renewable electricity.

The Old Faithful geyser in Yellowstone National Park in Wyoming has erupted every hour for at least 100 years.

Swimmers enjoy the Blue Lagoon hot spring in Iceland.

03 A volcanic, **igneous rock** called pumice can float on water. It is the only rock that can do this. Pumice is full of holes caused by gas bubbles in the molten rock. As the rock cools and hardens, the air is trapped inside, so the rock is light.

pumice

04 The sound from Krakatoa reportedly reached further than any other sound in history. Over 100 miles (160 km) away, the sound was as loud as an airplane taking off!

05 There is evidence that animals may be able to detect when an earthquake is coming, long before humans can. Elephants in Thailand ran to high ground hours before the 2004 tsunami happened.

VOLCANOES IN SPACE

Volcanoes exist on many of the planets and moons in our solar system, not just on Earth. Like Earth, these planets and moons have a mantle of molten rock, which may be forced to the surface as a volcano. Mars has many extinct volcanoes. One of these is Olympus Mons, which is the largest volcano in the solar system. It is a shield volcano, roughly the size of Germany, and is almost 16 miles (25 km) high. That's three times higher than Mount Everest!

Io is one of Jupiter's moons. In 1979, the *Voyager 1* spacecraft recorded the first pictures of a volcano erupting in space when it passed over Io. Jupiter's volcanoes spew out sulfur dioxide.

Venus has volcanoes called pancake domes. Viewed from space, they look just like pancakes and were formed when runny lava spread out, exactly like making pancakes in a frying pan!

GLOSSARY

archaeologist a historian who studies ruins and ancient objects to learn about historical people and events

avalanche a large, often dangerous, mass of snow, ice, or rock that falls away and travels down a mountain

dense tightly packed

erupt to burst out of the ground

evacuate to move away from an area to escape danger

geyser a hot spring that shoots out steam or hot water

glacier a large mass of ice, moving slowly down a mountain or spreading out on a land surface

igneous rock rock made by the action of intense heat, formed when lava cools

landslide a large amount of earth and rock sliding down hillsides or mountains

mineral a natural, useful, and sometimes valuable substance, often obtained from the ground

molten melted into a liquid by heat

nuclear plant a power station that collects nuclear energy

radioactive giving off a harmful type of energy called radiation

renewable able to be replaced by natural processes

satellite a machine in space that travels around planets, takes photographs, and collects information

sulfur dioxide a poisonous gas released by some volcanoes

supervolcano a giant volcanic eruption which releases more than 240 cubic miles (1,000 cubic km) of volcanic material

tremor a shaking or trembling movement

upwind against the direction of the wind

INDEX